PIONEER VALLEY EDUCATIONAL

WHAT TIME IS IT?

RUTH MATTISON

Here is a clock.
What time is it?

It is six o'clock.

Look at this clock.
What time is it?

It is eight o'clock.

Here is a clock.
This is a digital clock.
What time is it?

It is twelve o'clock.

Look at this clock.
What time is it?

It is one o'clock.

Here is a clock.
What time is it?

It is five o'clock.

Look at this clock.
What time is it?

It is two o'clock.

Here is a clock.
What time is it?

It is nine o'clock.

GLOSSARY

Twelve o'clock

One o'clock

Two o'clock

Five o'clock

Six o'clock

Eight o'clock

Nine o'clock

16